Welcome to the *Beyond Behaviors Flip Chart*

This flip chart offers therapists, teachers, and childhood providers a visual aid for understanding a child's behavioral challenges. It is based on the neurodevelopmental approach described in my award-winning book, *Beyond Behaviors*. While the flip chart can be used on its own, I recommend reading the book for additional tools, techniques, and worksheets—and for a more foundational understanding of child development and the neuroscience underlying the *Beyond Behaviors* approach.

Each page of the flip chart features a front-facing laminated side, in color, that presents a topic's essential ideas. You may want to use a dry-erase marker on this page to emphasize key points or to fill in information about each child. On the back side of each page, you'll find a black-and-white mirror image of the front, with additional instructional content for the presenter, whether it be a therapist, teacher, or parent. This page provides a useful visual guide to understand behaviors in the context of each child's individual differences, nervous system, and social-emotional development.

Ultimately, this flip chart will provide you with a new framework and lens for supporting children with behavioral challenges. I hope you enjoy using it!

— Mona Delahooke, PhD

Revealing the Hidden, Adaptive Benefits of Behaviors

In my clinical work, I've found that perpetually challenging behaviors in children are **rarely caused by intentional, willful defiance, avoidance, or manipulation.** Yet most educational approaches for persistent or severe behavioral problems are based on the assumption that they are. We respond to the behaviors with rewards or consequences in an attempt to promote more positive actions, driven by the belief that positive reinforcement or negative consequences improve compliance and reduce problematic behaviors.

But there's a new way to look at children's behavioral challenges. Instead of using reinforcement schedules, punishments, time-outs, and other such practices, we replace these techniques with a compassionate, neuroscience-based approach to support children with challenging behaviors.

The *Beyond Behaviors* approach shows how to understand behavioral challenges in a new way by considering how behaviors can be adaptive and protective to a child's nervous system.

Revealing the Hidden, Adaptive Benefits of Behaviors

In my clinical work, I've found that perpetually challenging behaviors in children are **rarely caused by intentional, willful defiance, avoidance, or manipulation.** Yet most educational approaches for persistent or severe behavioral problems are based on the assumption that they are. We respond to the behaviors with rewards or consequences in an attempt to promote more positive actions, driven by the belief that positive reinforcement or negative consequences improve compliance and reduce problematic behaviors.

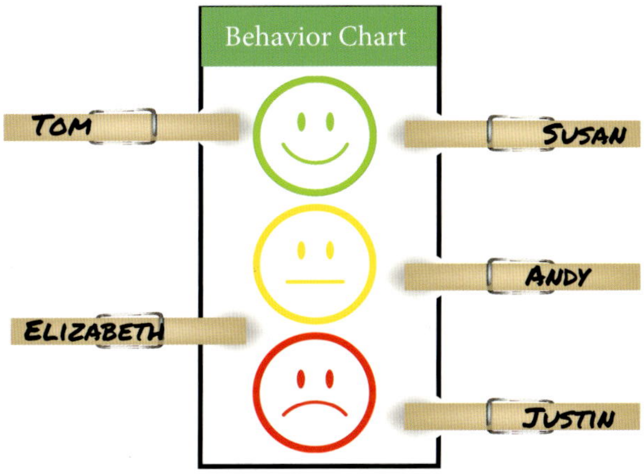

But there's a new way to look at children's behavioral challenges. Instead of using reinforcement schedules, punishments, time-outs, and other such practices, we replace these techniques with a compassionate, neuroscience-based approach to support children with challenging behaviors.

The *Beyond Behaviors* approach shows how to understand behavioral challenges in a new way by considering how behaviors can be adaptive and protective to a child's nervous system.

The Paradigm or Lens Shift

In traditional educational and psychology models, challenging or disruptive behaviors are often viewed as maladaptive—as if they reflect symptoms of a mental health diagnosis or a child's intention to misbehave. In reality, **all behaviors provide valuable clues about a child's individual differences, their social-emotional development, and the state of their autonomic nervous system.**

When we see a behavior that is problematic or confusing, the first question we ask shouldn't be "How do we get rid of it?" but rather "What is this telling us about the child?"

We discover the answer to this question by getting to know the child in a new way: by focusing not on the behaviors themselves **but on what underlies them**. This is a **lens or paradigm shift** in which we move from thinking about behaviors as the target of our intervention. We move beyond the idea that children are behaving in a certain way to get something, to get out of something, or to gain negative attention. Instead, we understand that behaviors are adaptive to a child's lived experience in the brain and body.

That means that instead of targeting behaviors for change, we look for the underlying reasons for the behaviors. That's where we aim our efforts to support each child.

The Paradigm or Lens Shift

In traditional educational and psychology models, challenging or disruptive behaviors are often viewed as maladaptive—as if they reflect symptoms of a mental health diagnosis or a child's intention to misbehave.

When we see a behavior that is problematic or confusing, the first question we ask shouldn't be "How do we get rid of it?" but rather "What is this telling us about the child?"

In reality, all behaviors provide valuable clues about a child's individual differences, their social-emotional development, and the state of their autonomic nervous system.

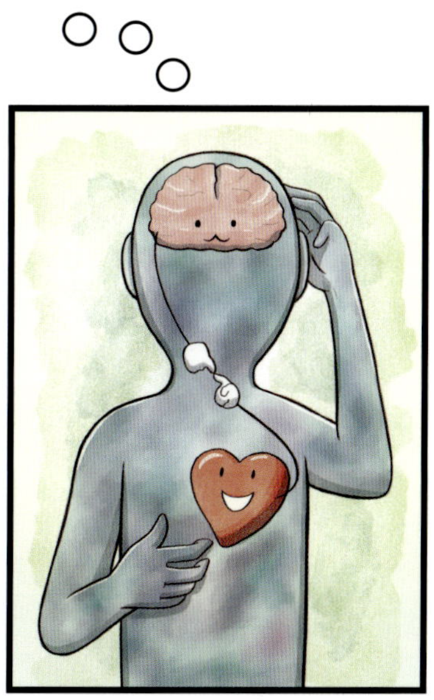

We View Behaviors as the Tip of the Iceberg

Behaviors are only the tip of the iceberg, so we need to look deeper to truly help children in a comprehensive way. The tip reveals the answer to the "what" questions about a person. As with an iceberg, below the surface is a much larger piece, concealed from view, but far more significant. Hidden here is the valuable information that can help us understand the "why" of a child's behaviors, including rich clues about possible causes and triggers.

Above the waterline, notice the different ways we tend to describe behaviors. Below the waterline, we see examples of triggers, or causes, of behaviors.

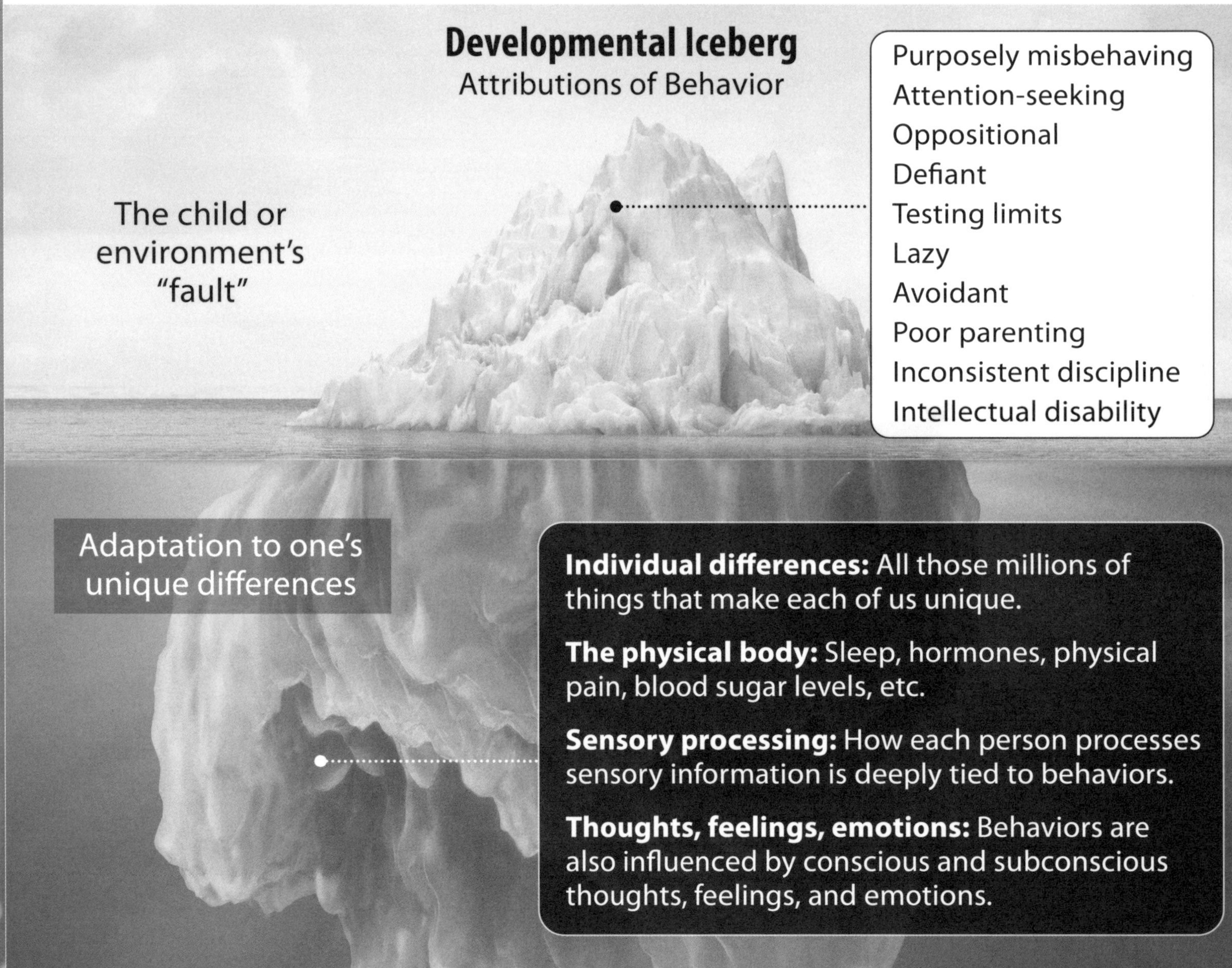

We View Behaviors as the Tip of the Iceberg

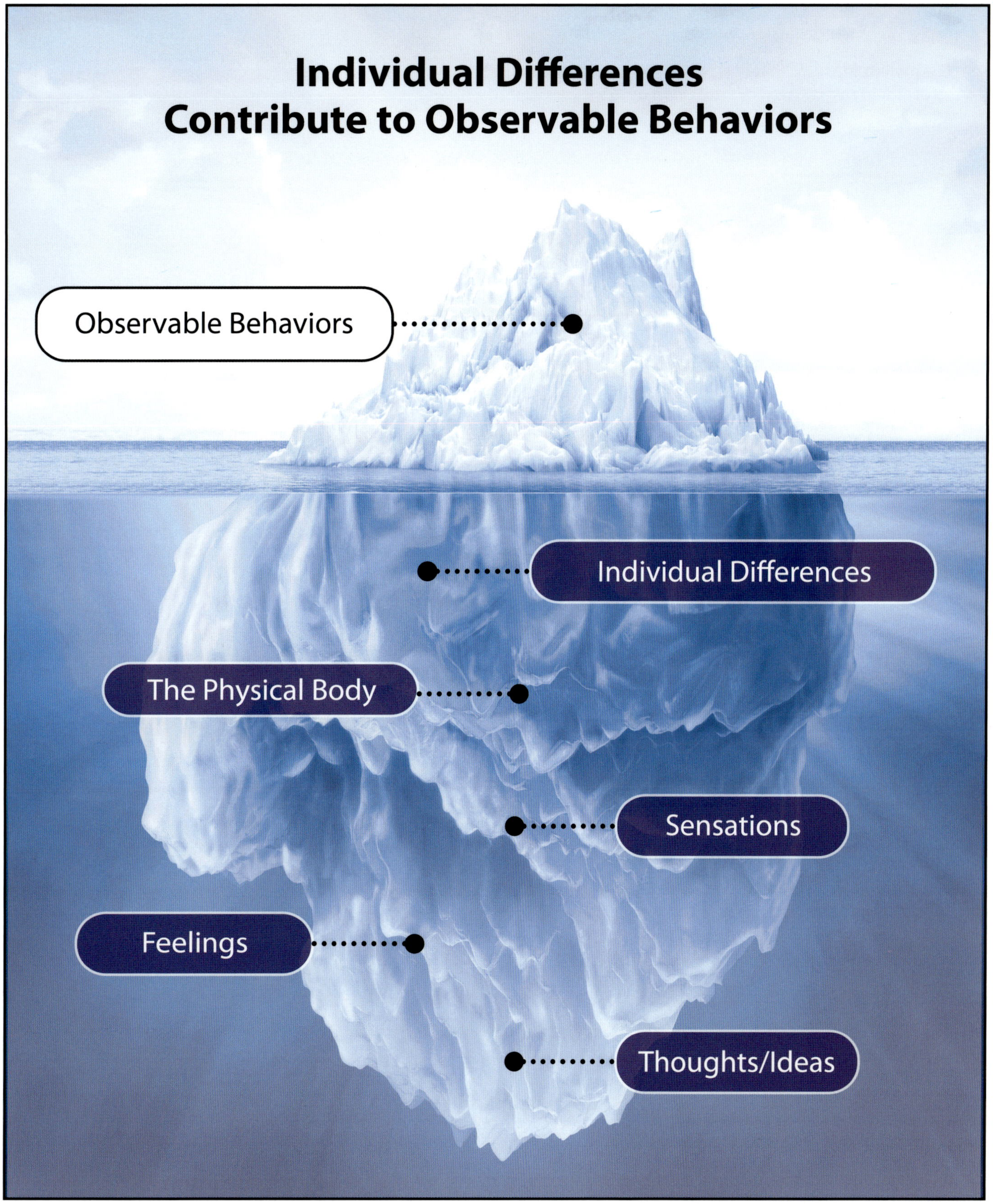

Looking Beneath the Tip of the Iceberg

We can view behavioral challenges through a new and expanded lens, a perspective informed by a dynamic synthesis of three areas:

① An understanding of the **autonomic nervous system** through the lens of Polyvagal Theory, a theory about the adaptive history of the autonomic nervous system (Porges, 2011)

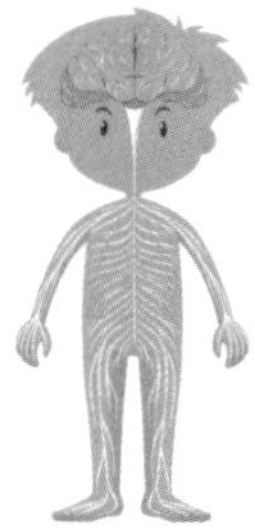

② A child's **social-emotional development** as described by the groundbreaking work of Stanley Greenspan and Serena Wieder, who developed the DIR (Developmental, Individual Difference, Relationship-Based) framework (Greenspan & Wieder, 1998)

③ An appreciation of each child's **individual differences**

Each of these three aspects helps us understand how we can best meet a child's **biological** and **emotional** needs, which underlie the behaviors we observe.

Essentially, the visceral state (our body's physiological state) influences children's behaviors and reactions to help them cope with their unique experience of being in the world.

Let's look at these three areas, but first, let's learn how a child's or adult's body knows how to direct movement, which results in the behaviors we see through a process called **neuroception**.

Looking Beneath the Tip of the Iceberg

We can view behavioral challenges through a new and expanded lens, a perspective informed by a dynamic synthesis of three areas:

1. An understanding of the autonomic nervous system through the lens of Polyvagal Theory

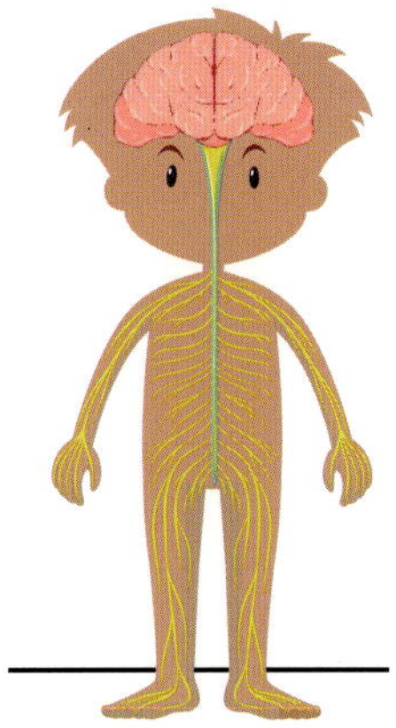

2. A child's social-emotional development

3. An appreciation of individual differences

What Directs Behaviors? Neuroception

Fortunately, we don't need to will our heart to beat or remind ourselves to breathe and digest our food; those things happen automatically.

There's also something else that happens automatically to help us stay safe. It's called **neuroception** (Porges, 2004).

Neuroception is "the process by which our nervous system evaluates risk without requiring awareness."

It's like an airport TSA agent or a computer antivirus program that constantly runs in the background, responding to cues of safety and threat in the environment, including the physical environment and the people around us.

The neuroception of safety is not equal to the absence of harm. A child may feel unsafe in an objectively "safe" classroom because the child's nervous system is picking up threat from the buzz of an air conditioner or fluorescent lighting, or from the emotional tone of a dysregulated classmate.

All sorts of things can help us experience the neuroception of **safety** (e.g., receiving a hug from a friend, playing, dancing, or listening to music we enjoy) or the neuroception of **threat** (e.g., hearing unexpected or uncomfortable sounds, seeing an angry stare, being isolated, being ignored, or feeling sick).

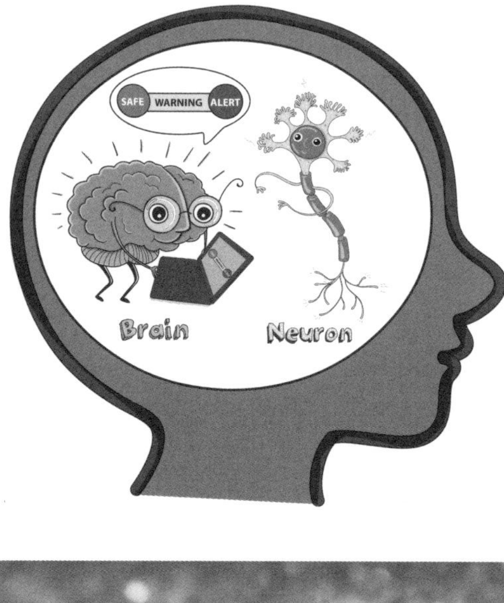

What Directs Behaviors? Neuroception

Fortunately, we don't need to will our heart to beat or remind ourselves to breathe and digest our food; those things happen automatically.

There's also something else that happens automatically to help us stay safe. It's called **neuroception** (Porges, 2004).

Neuroception is "the process by which our nervous system evaluates risk without requiring awareness."

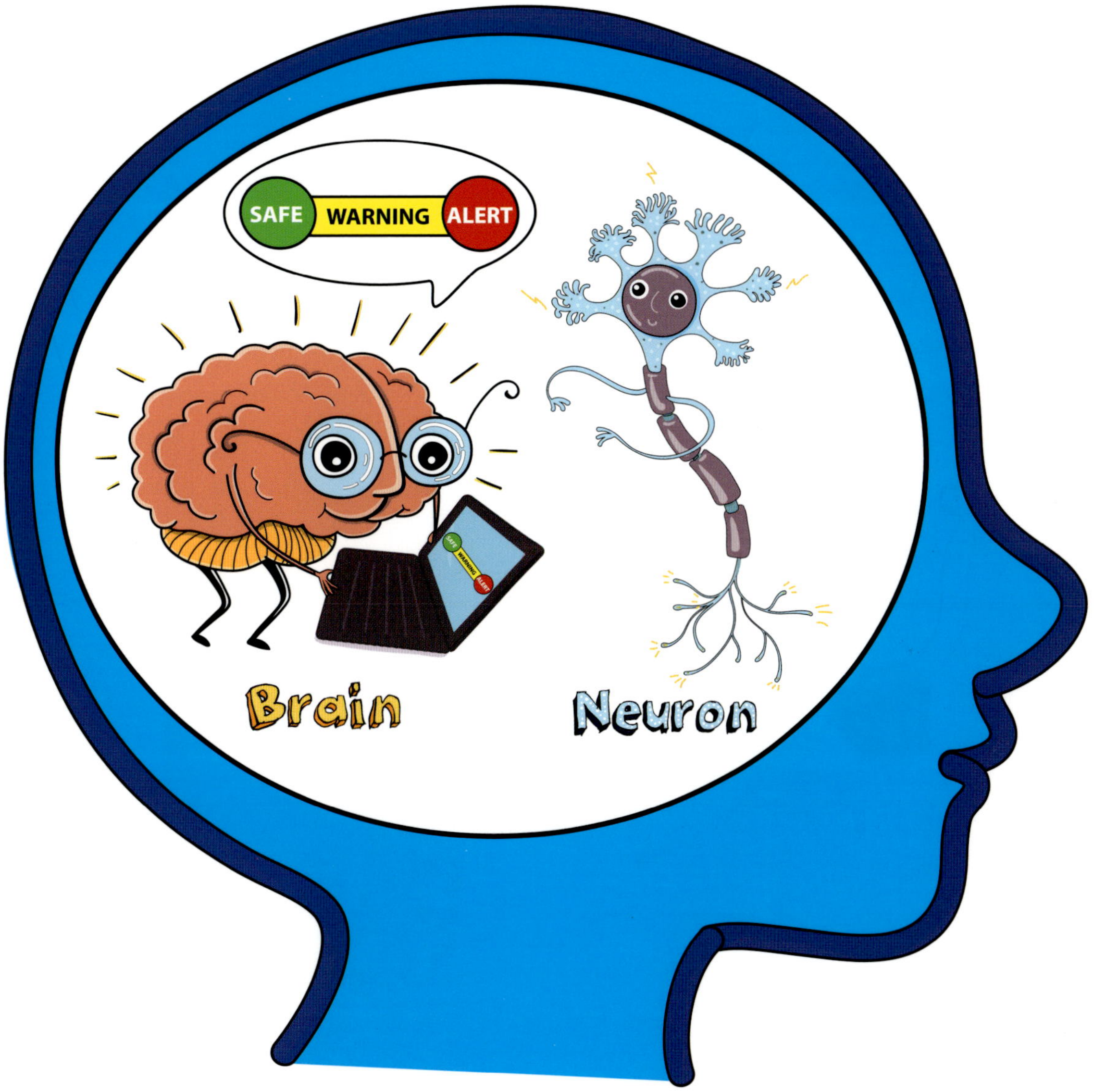

Understanding the Autonomic Nervous System through the Lens of Polyvagal Theory

Many professionals use color systems to teach individuals how to develop self-regulation and emotional control.

The *Beyond Behaviors* approach also uses colors but in a much different way: not to teach children, **but for adults to learn about the child's (and their own) autonomic state in real time.**

The green, red, and blue colors represent the activation of three main autonomic pathways of responses defined by the Polyvagal Theory as described by Lillas & Turnbull (2009).

The GREEN PATHWAY is the **VENTRAL VAGAL SYSTEM**, which supports social engagement and connection under the conditions of relational and environmental safety.

The RED PATHWAY is the **SYMPATHETIC NERVOUS SYSTEM**, which supports survival through mobilization, commonly known as the fight-or-flight response.

The BLUE PATHWAY is the **DORSAL VAGAL SYSTEM**, which helps us protect ourselves against life threat by immobilizing and shutting down.

We can make educated guesses about a child's autonomic state by observing their body and behaviors. The checklists on the next several pages can help us determine which pathway the child (or adult) is on.

Understanding the Autonomic Nervous System through the Lens of Polyvagal Theory

Many professionals use color systems to teach individuals how to develop self-regulation and emotional control.

The *Beyond Behaviors* approach also uses colors but in a much different way: not to teach children, **but for adults to learn about the child's (and their own) autonomic state in real time.**

The green, red, and blue colors represent the activation of three main autonomic pathways of responses defined by the Polyvagal Theory as described by Lillas & Turnbull (2009).

The **GREEN PATHWAY** is the **VENTRAL VAGAL SYSTEM**, which supports social engagement and connection under the conditions of relational and environmental safety.

The **RED PATHWAY** is the **SYMPATHETIC NERVOUS SYSTEM**, which supports survival through mobilization, commonly known as the fight-or-flight response.

The **BLUE PATHWAY** is the **DORSAL VAGAL SYSTEM**, which helps us protect ourselves against life threat by immobilizing and shutting down.

Green Pathway – Social Engagement

Eyes

- ☐ Bright, shiny eyes
- ☐ Looks directly at people, objects
- ☐ Looks away for breaks, then returns to eye contact
- ☐ Seems alert, takes in information

Face

- ☐ Smiles, shows joy
- ☐ Neutral
- ☐ Can express all emotions

Body

- ☐ Relaxed with good muscle tone
- ☐ Stable, balanced and coordinated movements
- ☐ Infant moves arms and legs toward center of the body
- ☐ Infant molds body into a caregiver when held
- ☐ Moves faster or slower depending on environment

Rhythm/Rate of Movement

- ☐ Changes smoothly to respond to the environment
- ☐ Movements not too fast or too slow

Voice

- ☐ Laughing
- ☐ Tone changes

Green Pathway – Social Engagement

Eyes

- ☐ Bright, shiny eyes
- ☐ Looks directly at people, objects
- ☐ Looks away for breaks, then returns to eye contact
- ☐ Seems alert, takes in information

Face

- ☐ Smiles, shows joy
- ☐ Neutral
- ☐ Can express all emotions

Body

- ☐ Relaxed with good muscle tone
- ☐ Stable, balanced and coordinated movements
- ☐ Infant moves arms and legs toward center of the body
- ☐ Infant molds body into a caregiver when held
- ☐ Moves faster or slower depending on environment

Rhythm/Rate of Movement

- ☐ Changes smoothly to respond to the environment
- ☐ Movements not too fast or too slow

Voice

- ☐ Laughing
- ☐ Tone changes

Red Pathway – Fight or Flight

Body

- ☐ Fingers spread out
- ☐ Arched back, tense body position
- ☐ Constant motion
- ☐ Demands space by pushing, shoving, and getting into others' space
- ☐ Biting, hitting, kicking, jumping, throwing
- ☐ Bumps into things, falls
- ☐ Threatening gestures (shakes finger or fist)

Eyes

- ☐ Open, squinted, or closed eyes
- ☐ May have direct, intense eye contact
- ☐ Eyes roll upward
- ☐ Eyes look quickly around the room

Rhythm/Rate of Movement

- ☐ Fast movements
- ☐ Impulsive movements

Face

- ☐ Wide-open mouth
- ☐ Anger, disgust
- ☐ Frown, grimace
- ☐ Fake, forced smile
- ☐ Clenched jaw or teeth

Voice

- ☐ High-pitched crying, yelling, or screaming
- ☐ Loud
- ☐ Hostile or grumpy
- ☐ Sarcastic
- ☐ Out-of-control laughing

Red Pathway – Fight or Flight

Eyes

- ☐ Open, squinted, or closed eyes
- ☐ May have direct, intense eye contact
- ☐ Eyes roll upward
- ☐ Eyes look quickly around the room

Face

- ☐ Wide-open mouth
- ☐ Anger, disgust
- ☐ Frown, grimace
- ☐ Fake, forced smile
- ☐ Clenched jaw or teeth

Body

- ☐ Fingers spread out
- ☐ Arched back, tense body position
- ☐ Constant motion
- ☐ Demands space by pushing, shoving, and getting into others' space
- ☐ Biting, hitting, kicking, jumping, throwing
- ☐ Bumps into things, falls
- ☐ Threatening gestures (shakes finger or fist)

Rhythm/Rate of Movement

- ☐ Fast movements
- ☐ Impulsive movements

Voice

- ☐ High-pitched crying, yelling, or screaming
- ☐ Loud
- ☐ Hostile or grumpy
- ☐ Sarcastic
- ☐ Out-of-control laughing

Blue Pathway – Shutting Down

Eyes

- ☐ Glazed/glassy eyes (looks through rather than at)
- ☐ Looks away for a long time, looks down
- ☐ Seems drowsy/tired
- ☐ Does not look around the room for interesting items
- ☐ Looks at things more than people

Face

- ☐ Flat/blank
- ☐ Mouth turned down, sad

Body

- ☐ Slumped/slouching
- ☐ Low muscle tone
- ☐ Little or no exploring play or curiosity
- ☐ Wanders
- ☐ Frozen or slow-moving

Rhythm/Rate of Movement

- ☐ Slow movements
- ☐ Slow to start moving

Voice

- ☐ Flat
- ☐ Makes few to no sounds
- ☐ Sounds cold, soft, sad, too quiet

Blue Pathway – Shutting Down

Eyes

- ☐ Glazed/glassy eyes (looks through rather than at)
- ☐ Looks away for a long time, looks down
- ☐ Seems drowsy/tired
- ☐ Does not look around the room for interesting items
- ☐ Looks at things more than people

Face

- ☐ Flat/blank
- ☐ Mouth turned down, sad

Body

- ☐ Slumped/slouching
- ☐ Low muscle tone
- ☐ Little or no exploring play or curiosity
- ☐ Wanders
- ☐ Frozen or slow-moving

Rhythm/Rate of Movement

- ☐ Slow movements
- ☐ Slow to start moving

Voice

- ☐ Flat
- ☐ Makes few to no sounds
- ☐ Sounds cold, soft, sad, too quiet

What Directs Behaviors? A Child's Social-Emotional Development

Greenspan and Wieder (1998) describe six main processes of social-emotional development that impact behavioral and emotional control. A simplified way to look at these six processes is to compare them to building a house. We can evaluate where a child is in general or in the moment by asking the following questions:

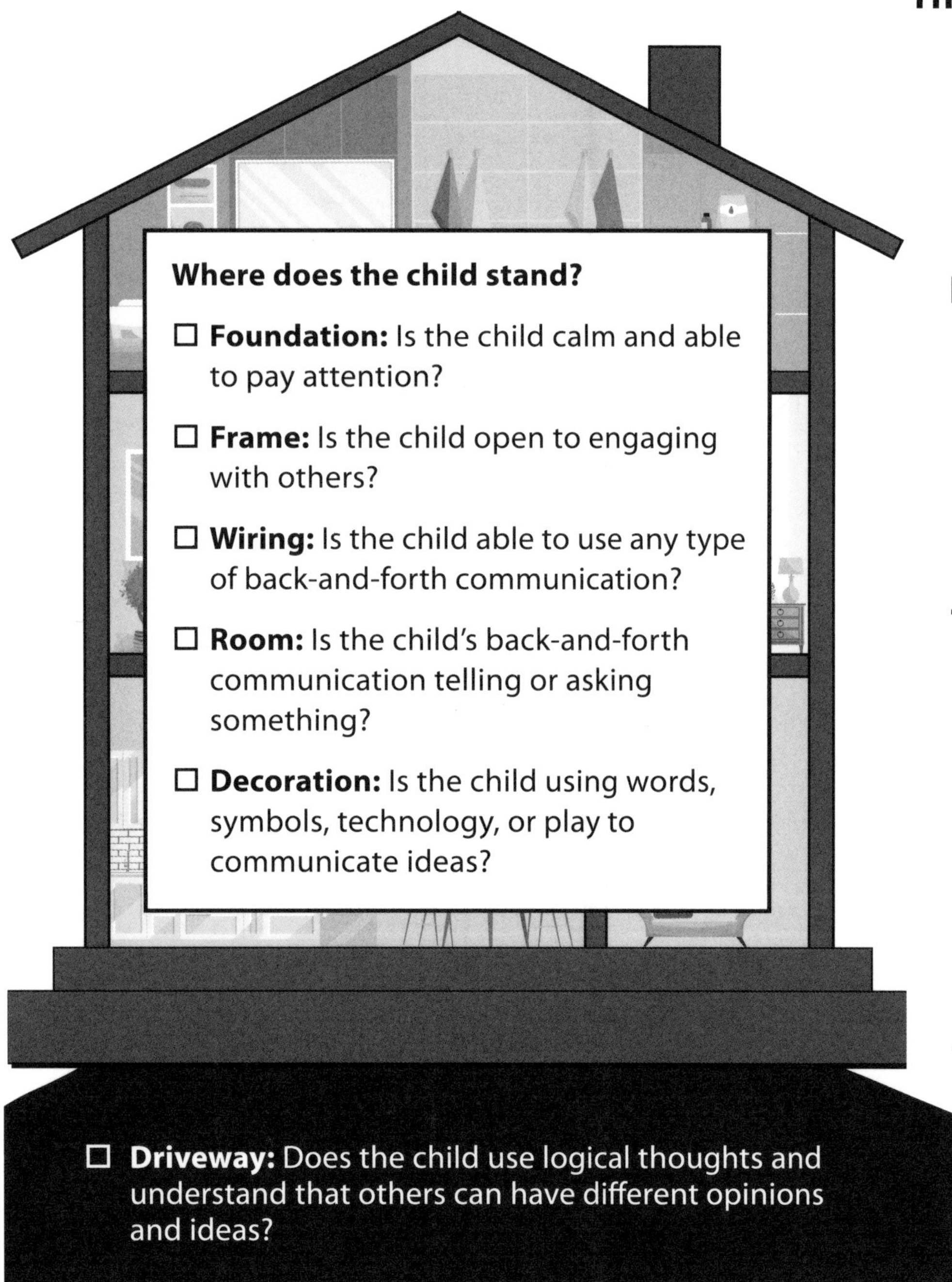

The Foundation of the House
Process (1):
Regulation and Attention

Framing the House
Process (2):
Engagement and Relating

The Electrical Wiring
Process (3):
Purposeful Emotional Interactions

The Rooms of the House
Process (4):
Social Problem-Solving

Decorating the House
Process (5):
Creating Symbols and Using Words and Ideas

The Driveway to the World
Process (6):
Emotional Thinking and Building Bridges Between Ideas

What Directs Behaviors? A Child's Social-Emotional Development

Where does the child stand?

- ☐ **Foundation:** Is the child calm and able to pay attention?
- ☐ **Frame:** Is the child open to engaging with others?
- ☐ **Wiring:** Is the child able to use any type of back-and-forth communication?
- ☐ **Room:** Is the child's back-and-forth communication telling or asking something?
- ☐ **Decoration:** Is the child using words, symbols, technology, or play to communicate ideas?

- ☐ **Driveway:** Does the child use logical thoughts and understand that others can have different opinions and ideas?

What Directs Behaviors? Individual Differences

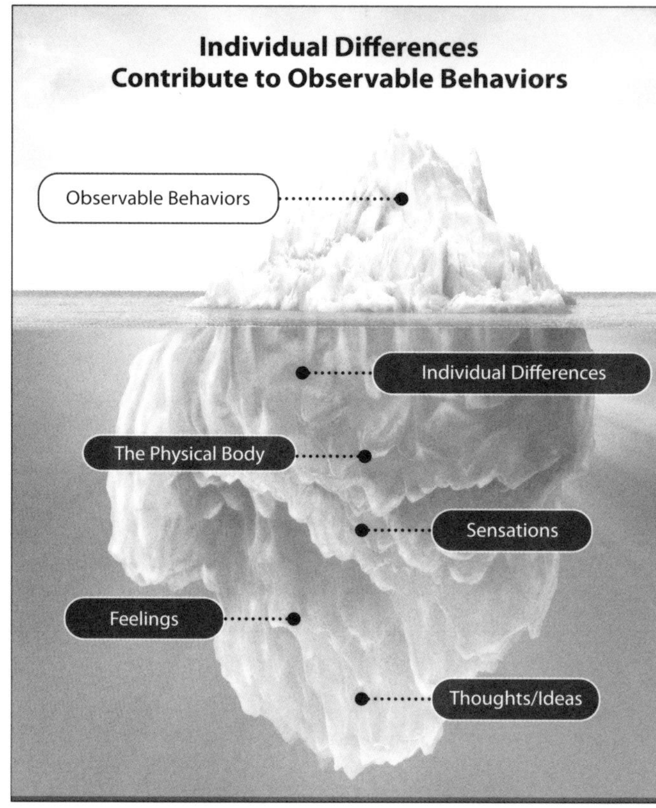

This iceberg explains the four large categories of causes and triggers, which involve individual differences in:

- **The physical body:** Lack of restful sleep, hunger, illness, fatigue, relational or environmental stress, and anything else that impacts the body can affect a child's basic health.

- **Sensory processing:** Sometimes, the behaviors we see are a child's body's way of coping with sensory challenges. By understanding a child's sensory processing—how that child interprets the world through their senses—we can better understand the reasons for these behaviors. Sometimes, over- or under-reactivity in one or more of the sensory channels contributes to a child's early behavioral and emotional disruption. With the help of an occupational therapist who is familiar with sensory processing, ask if the child might be over- or under-reactive, or craving of sensations.

- **Emotions:** Feedback loops between the body and the brain compel the body to move, influencing our feelings and emotions, as well as the behaviors we see (Porges, 2011).

- **Thoughts:** Our behaviors can also be caused by the thoughts we have and by how we make meaning out of our current experiences based on our past experiences.

Let's consider together what's underneath ________________'s [*child's name*] iceberg.

Note: Chapter 3 in *Beyond Behaviors* contains a variety of checklists you can use with parents or caregivers to ascertain the contribution of sensory processing differences to a child's behaviors and emotions.

What Directs Behaviors? Individual Differences

Developmental Iceberg

Attributions of Behavior

Identifying the Causes and Triggers of Behavioral Challenges

Let's now use the information we have gathered about these three areas to best support the child's behavioral challenges:

①	②	③
A child's nervous system and how safe they feel in their body (The Colors)	Individual differences (The Iceberg)	Social-emotional development (The House)

This approach allows us to work on the level of the triggers and causes of the behavioral challenges, rather than on surface behaviors.

Let's start with filling in the developmental iceberg. Using a dry-erase marker, list the child's behavioral challenges on the top and the potential triggers or causes on the bottom.

Remember to consider:

- Contributions from the **physical body** that can impact a child's basic health
- How the child interprets the world through their various **senses**
- The child's **social and emotional processes** (the "house")
- The **emotional environment** and the child's emotional state
- The **thoughts and beliefs** that might be at play in instructing the child's actions

Identifying the Causes and Triggers of Behavioral Challenges

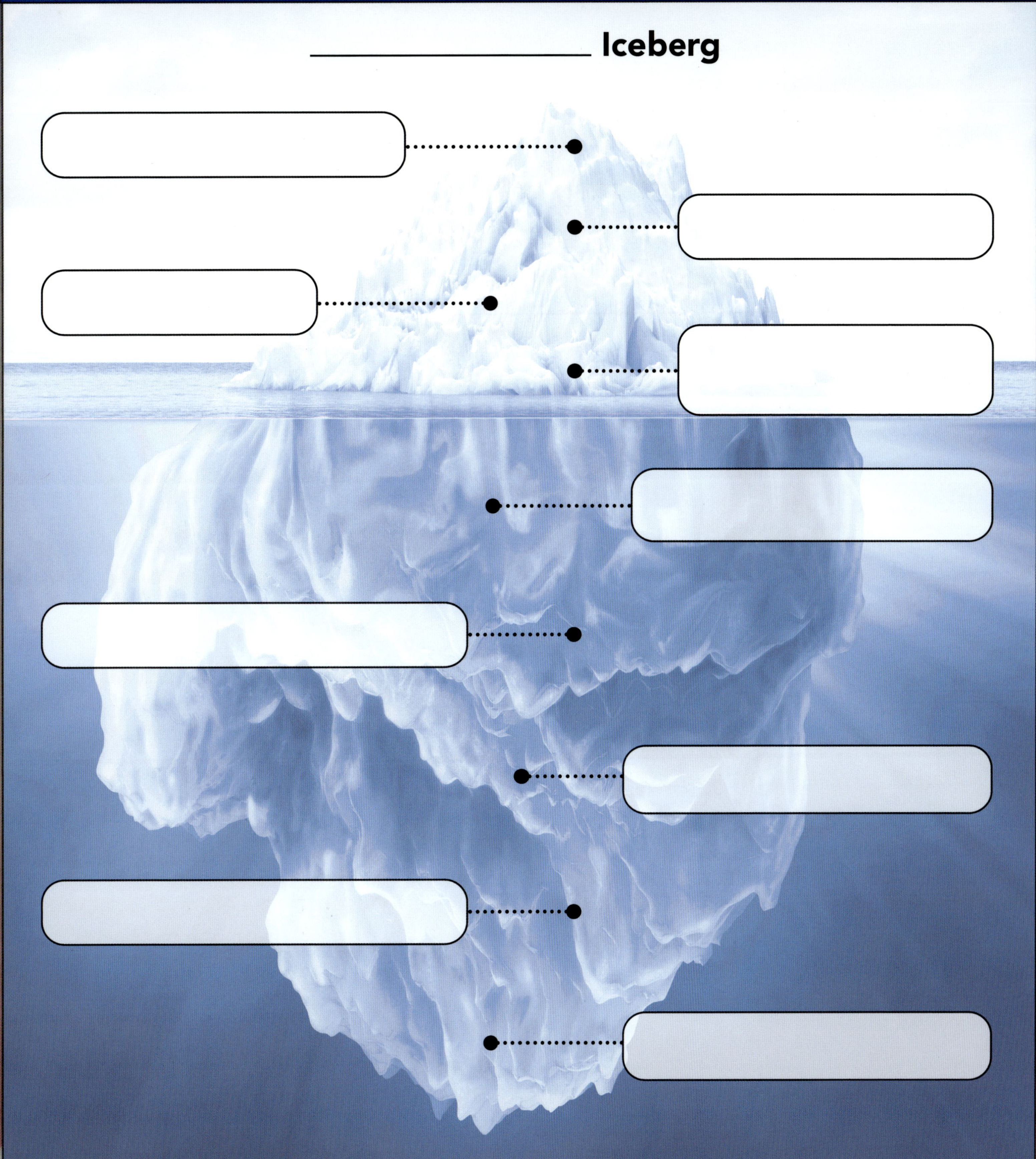

Social & Emotional Check-In

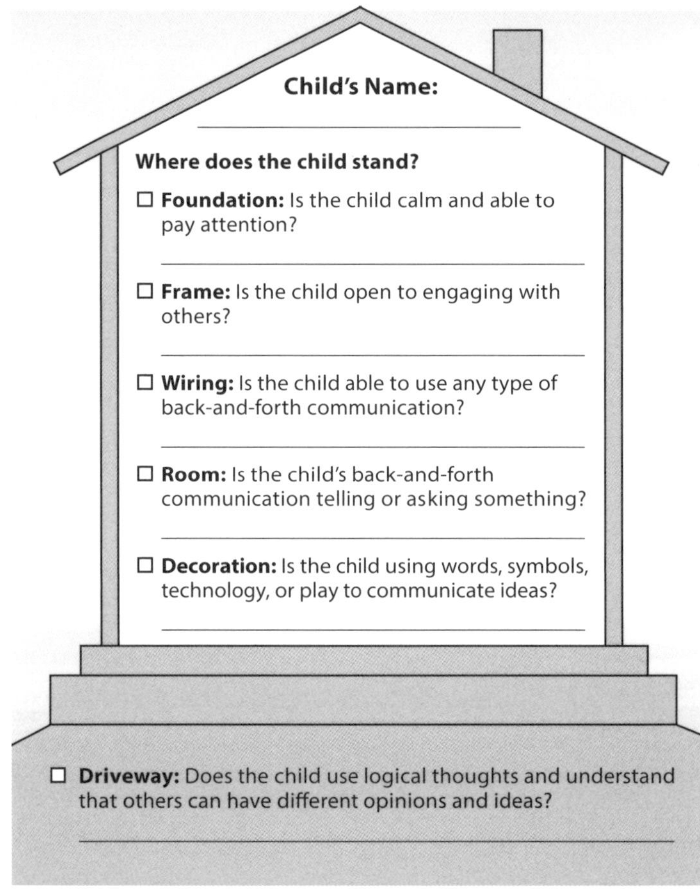

- Even though most children begin to have "effortful control" of their behaviors, emotions, attention, and impulses in toddlerhood, it takes many years for these abilities to develop fully—even through early adulthood.

- As social-emotional development grows, children develop greater **top-down** thinking skills, as well as the ability to learn and reflect on their actions.

- **Bottom-up** or instinctual and protective behaviors are reflexive and self-protective, and they don't involve conscious thought. When children are still developing capacities in the first four processes (i.e., foundation, frame, wiring, rooms), they will exhibit more bottom-up behaviors because their ability to control their emotions and behaviors—and to use self-talk and reasoning to regulate—are still under construction.

- Look again at the six processes of the social-emotional house, and reflect on each of the six parts of the house. Where is ________________ [*child's name*] now? Is there a difference in each category at home and other places, like school? Check the boxes and use different colored dry-erase markers for different locations.

- Where does ________________ [*child's name*] need to grow, starting from the earliest, most important foundation: the ability to regulate in the physical body? How sturdy is that first milestone?

Social & Emotional Check-In

Child's Name:

____

Where does the child stand?

☐ **Foundation:** Is the child calm and able to pay attention?

____

☐ **Frame:** Is the child open to engaging with others?

____

☐ **Wiring:** Is the child able to use any type of back-and-forth communication?

____

☐ **Room:** Is the child's back-and-forth communication telling or asking something?

____

☐ **Decoration:** Is the child using words, symbols, technology, or play to communicate ideas?

____

☐ **Driveway:** Does the child use logical thoughts and understand that others can have different opinions and ideas?

____

Plan for ______________________

[*Child's Name*]

- List the concerning behaviors.

- List the "reframe" from misbehavior to adaptation (e.g., Johnny's need to move about the classroom is an adaptation to a sensory need, not a purposeful misbehavior).

- List the triggers or causes that may underlie the child's (protective) stress behaviors (e.g., sensory processing challenges, insufficient relational support from teachers or staff, social-emotional differences, problems with peers, physical discomfort, stress resulting from separation from the safety of their caregiver or home environment).

- List the social-emotional supports to be put in place for the child (e.g., teacher, aides, or caregivers will comfort the child and provide emotional support, will pay attention to the need underlying the stress behaviors rather than ignoring "noncompliant" behaviors, will support joyful peer or sibling interactions, and will play with the child).

- List the environmental adjustments or accommodations that can provide additional support (e.g., provide noise-canceling headphones for auditory sensitivities, place the child's chair in closer proximity to caring adults for relational security, monitor noise and visual distractions in the classroom, allow the child the opportunity to move their body as needed).

Plan for ______________________________

[*Child's Name*]

- List the concerning behaviors:

____

____

- List the "reframe" from misbehavior to adaptation:

____

____

- List the triggers or causes that may underlie the child's (protective) stress behaviors:

____

____

- List the social-emotional supports to be put in place for the child:

____

____

- List the environmental adjustments or necessary accommodations that can provide additional support:

____

____

- We can best support a child when we are calm ourselves. **It's important to be aware that the state of our nervous system impacts a child's nervous system.** Therefore, the first step when we attune to a child who is struggling is not telling, teaching, or instructing. **It is being warmly attuned and present with the child.** *How* we say things is as important as what we say. Consider the cues of safety that all adults around the child are providing.
- When we offer this kind of help, we're engaging in emotional **co-regulation** by supporting another person through our presence. This expands a child's tolerance for new experiences, sensations, feelings, and ideas. It also results in fewer behavioral challenges. Consider the messages the child is receiving from the adults in their life.

Providing Cues of Relational Safety for Children

According to the Polyvagal perspective, humans provide cues of safety or threat through tone of voice, facial expressions, posture, and other nonverbal forms of communication.

Consider: Am I working off of an emotionally stable platform? Are the cues I am providing the child supportive of social engagement? Use the following questions to gauge your use of safety cues and check off those that apply to you.

Presence: Am I present with the child, attending to them singularly, and not distracted or multitasking?

Tone of voice: Is the volume of my voice appropriate to the child's needs? Is there inflection or prosody in my voice? Is there warmth and a caring tone to my voice?

Facial expression: Is my face expressive of safety and engagement?

Pacing and timing: Am I approaching and pacing with the child in accordance to their immediate needs?

Posture: Do I have a relaxed posture and inviting gestures?

Adult Checklist

Providing Cues of Relational Safety for Children

According to the Polyvagal perspective, humans provide cues of safety or threat through tone of voice, facial expressions, posture, and other nonverbal forms of communication.

Consider: Am I working off of an emotionally stable platform? Are the cues I am providing the child supportive of social engagement? Use the following questions to gauge your use of safety cues and check off those that apply to you.

Presence:

______ Am I present with the child, attending to them singularly, and not distracted or multitasking?

Tone of voice:

______ Is the volume of my voice appropriate to the child's needs?

______ Is there inflection or prosody in my voice?

______ Is there warmth and a caring tone to my voice?

Facial expression:

______ Is my face expressive of safety and engagement?

Pacing and timing:

______ Am I approaching and pacing with the child in accordance to their immediate needs?

Posture:

______ Do I have a relaxed posture and inviting gestures?

Co-regulation Through Play

If a child is working on gaining abilities in the first four processes of the house—regulation, engagement, back-and-forth communication, and social problem-solving—it's best to focus on what Dr. Porges calls the best possible neural exercise for children: **play**.

Child-led play is the best way to strengthen a child's growing capacities for emotional and behavioral control.

What kinds of play activities are most enjoyable for your child or student? Do you enjoy them as well?

Let's talk about the play basics that help children. Any amount of time is helpful, but consider chunks of at least 10 minutes to:

- Unplug and let go of all distractions.
- Have fun, relax, and stay curious.
- Follow the child's lead and value their play themes and needs.
- Let go of any agenda—just follow.
- Be interactive and engaged.
- Refrain from teaching or asking questions in play that you already know the answer to (e.g., "What color is the frog?").
- Become the characters and connect to your inner child.
- Have fun!

If the play themes that come up are concerning to you, or if you are unsure about how to play with your child, I recommend contacting a child therapist with a background in play-based interventions, such as DIR-Floortime or Child-Parent Psychotherapy (CPP). (See the last page of this flip chart for additional resources.)

Note: You can find a detailed description of how to use play to help children on their developmental journey in chapters 5 and 6 of *Beyond Behaviors*.

Co-regulation Through Play

Let's talk about the play basics that help children:

- Unplug and let go of all distractions.
- Have fun, relax, and stay curious.
- Follow the child's lead and value their play themes and needs.
- Let go of any agenda—just follow.
- Be interactive and engaged.
- Refrain from teaching or asking questions in play that you already know the answer to (e.g., "What color is the frog?").
- Become the characters and connect to your inner child.
- Have fun!

In many approaches to behavioral management, we don't use a developmental roadmap to help children with challenges. Instead, we try to teach first, before the child (or teenager) is capable of doing what's being taught.

But we need to wait to introduce top-down strategies until the child or teen is developmentally ready. Why? **Because we shouldn't require children to mobilize their own self-regulation strategies if they don't yet have that ability. Instead, we should engage and nurture them first through emotional co-regulation.**

In other words, **being with** the child comes before teaching the child.

Once a child has top-down abilities, they can use the incredible power of thinking to find effective ways to cope with challenges. This is what the field of mental health is built upon—the solid rock of interpersonal, healing exchanges that help individuals understand themselves better, reduce their own suffering, and find better ways to manage their difficult emotions.

Note: Only move on to the next page of the flip chart if the child or teen is developmentally able and comfortable using top-down thinking. Skip if not.

Helping to Build Top-Down Strategies

In many approaches to behavioral management, we don't use a developmental roadmap to help children with challenges. Instead, we try to teach first, before the child (or teenager) is capable of doing what's being taught.

But we shouldn't require children to mobilize their own self-regulation strategies if they don't yet have that ability. Instead, we should engage and nurture them first through emotional co-regulation.

In other words, **being with** the child comes before teaching the child.

Once a child has top-down abilities, they can use the incredible power of thinking to find effective ways to cope with challenges. This is what the field of mental health is built upon—the solid rock of interpersonal, healing exchanges that help individuals understand themselves better, reduce their own suffering, and find better ways to manage their difficult emotions.

Helping to Build Top-Down Strategies

This exercise is intended to help children devise coping strategies when managing stress-related changes in their nervous systems.

This sample narrative can help children identify the state of their nervous system in a simple way, which we can customize according to ___________'s [*client's name*] language level.

But remember: We shouldn't require children to mobilize their own self-regulation strategies until we engage and nurture them first through emotional co-regulation. Only once we sufficiently address this step do we help children identify the states of their nervous system.

Note: Chapter 6 of *Beyond Behaviors* provides a narrative exercise to help children develop ways to describe the three basic states of the nervous system—not with colors, but by choosing their own special words. I recommend using this chapter and exercise if the child needs more in-depth support to describe how their body feels, which can help the child figure out how to ask for what they need emotionally.

Helping to Build Top-Down Strategies

Here's a sample narrative you can use to help a child identify the state of their nervous system in a simple way:

When I'm feeling ______________________ [*child's word for big feelings*], I can get help or help myself get back to feeling ______________________ [*child's word for calm, cozy, and safe*] by doing these things:

____

____

____

____

When I'm feeling ______________________ [*child's word for sad, lonely, or slow*], I can get help or help myself get back to feeling ______________________ [*child's word for calm, cozy, and safe*] by doing these things:

____

____

____

____

Looking Beyond Behaviors

The *Beyond Behaviors* approach—in which we look first to the *underlying physiological and emotional meanings* behind the behaviors—is not yet widely implemented in education or mental health.

That's because this developmental approach involves the translation and integration of relational neuroscience into practice. Changes that integrate new science take a long time to implement into education, social work, juvenile justice, and mental health settings.

I created this flip chart as a friendly way to introduce the concepts that I hope will create a paradigm shift for supporting all children. I invite you to learn more on my website, www.monadelahooke.com, and on social media @monadelahooke.

I wish you and your child, student, or client well on this journey.

About the Author

Mona Delahooke, PhD, is a licensed clinical psychologist with more than thirty years of experience caring for children and their families. She is a senior faculty member of the Profectum Foundation and a member of the American Psychological Association.

She is the author of *Beyond Behaviors: Using Brain Science and Compassion to Understand and Solve Children's Behavioral Challenges* and *Brain-Body Parenting: How to Stop Managing Behavior and Start Raising Joyful, Resilient Kids*. Dr. Delahooke is a frequent speaker, trainer, and consultant to parents, organizations, schools, and public agencies. She lives and works in the Los Angeles area.

Additional Resources by Mona Delahooke, PhD

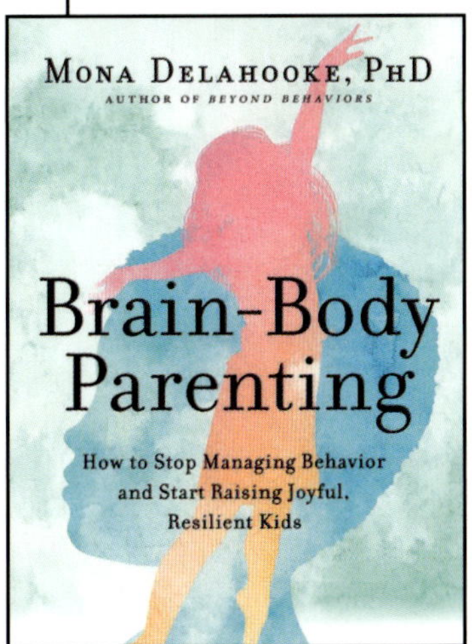

References

Delahooke, M. (2019). *Beyond behaviors: Using brain science and compassion to understand and solve children's behavioral challenges.* PESI Publishing.

Greenspan, S., & Wieder, S. (1998). *The child with special needs: Encouraging intellectual and emotional growth.* Perseus Books.

Lillas, C., & Turnbull, J. (2009). *Infant/child mental health, early intervention, and relationship-based therapies: A neurorelational framework for interdisciplinary practice.* W.W. Norton.

Porges, S. W. (2004). Neuroception: A subconscious system for detecting threats and safety. *Zero to Three*, *24*(5), 19–24.

Porges, S. W. (2011). *The polyvagal theory: Neurophysiological foundations of emotions, attachment, communication, and self-regulation*. W. W. Norton.